THE
ABUNDANT KITCHEN

Recipes from the culinary classroom
for the family home cook

BECKI MELVIE

Food Photography: All photos by Dennis Becker except, Chris Cline (pg. 22, 25, 26), Christine Fagerlie (pg. 18, 90), Adobe Stock, David Kadlec (pg. 56)

Food Styling: Lisa Golden-Schroeder

Illustrations: Lydia Hugh-Jones

ISBN 13: 978-1-64343-901-3

Library of Congress Catalog Number: 2020903256

Printed in Canada
First Printing: 2020
24 23 22 21 20   5 4 3 2 1

Cover and interior design by James Monroe Design, LLC.

BEAVER'S
POND
PRESS

Beaver's Pond Press, Inc.
939 Seventh Street West
Saint Paul, MN 55102
(952) 829-8818
www.BeaversPondPress.com

For T, C, and L
You inspire my best.

Two things I ask of you, deny them not to me before I die.
Remove from me falsehood and lying; give me neither riches nor poverty,
feed me with food that is needed for me.

—Proverbs 30:7-8

CONTENTS

Introduction // 1

INTRODUCTION

It was standing over a sink filled with dirty dishes on a cold January night that inspired my Google search for culinary schools. What could make my life complete? How could I be what I was intended to be? Maybe a chef with international culinary training? There was a school in Vermont. Another in Italy. Australia had a culinary program. There was the Culinary Institute of America (CIA) in San Francisco and New York. Minnesota had a couple of schools with four-year programs, but ugh, that seemed like a big-time commitment. Then I discovered Ballymaloe Cookery School (BCS), an organic farm with a chef training program in County Cork, Ireland. The prospect of learning on the hundred acres of gardens, which included cow pasture, an apple orchard, farm sheds, and chicken coops, immediately drew me in. I loved the idea of being completely immersed in learning where your food comes from. Although it was a place I'd never been before and I knew little about, it seemed so much like where I had grown up. My youth was spent eating green peppers like apples in my dad's lush, prolific garden, which flourished near the marsh where my brother and cousins hunted for duck. I spent my days walking the woods, looking for morels or beating my chest trying to draw in a pheasant. When I wasn't outside, I was perched near the stove during the harvest, listening to the high-pitched scream of my mom's pressure canner. Or I was in my grandmother Rita's kitchen on the pig farm in Darwin, Minnesota, learning how to properly level baking powder for Christmas cookies. More than anything, I wanted to make a go of sharing my lifelong passion for food with others. Ballymaloe Cookery School seemed like the perfect fit, and it would give me the authority in the culinary industry to pursue my dream.

When I broached the subject of moving to Ireland, my husband, Travis, shockingly responded with a full bodied "Yes!" So, Travis left his IT job of twenty years, and we began the daunting task of prepping and packing our lives into four suitcases for the trip of a lifetime. Our boys were small then, one four years old and the other seven, so this was no easy task.

During the twelve-week chef certificate program I completed, we were tasked with a rigorous training schedule. Mornings were practical cooking time. We were assigned a partner and recipes; we would divvy up the work between the two of us and share a cooking station. After completing the morning's cook, we would present the dishes to the instructor for our marks and hope for a ten. Then, all sixty-five students, representing seven countries, would serve lunch in the two separate dining rooms. The afternoon would consist of a seated lecture and demonstration about how to cook the next day's recipes.

School was tough, and at one point the pace became grueling. Learning all day, every day turned my head into mush. Some nights, instead of going to sleep, my mind would descend into a tailspin until three in the morning as I worked to process all the information learned that day. *Stollen cake! Monkfish filleting! Pain au chocolat! What is an oxtail? Producer of the week! Biscuit of the week! Gluten-free flours! How do you make a proper cup of tea? How is a caper grown? Where is the gullet?*

Being around the finest ingredients, sourced from the best locations in the world, with local produce grown organically in a microclimate close to the sea year-round, left me completely appreciative of truly one-of-a-kind cheffy ingredients. *Olive oil from the first pressing of the season in Tuscany! Valrhona chocolate! Spices directly from India! Quail eggs! Lobster caught that morning! Wines from Bordeaux, South Africa, and Australia! Sherry from Jerez! Port from Douro Valley! All the produce of the Wild Atlantic Way!*

My favorite things to learn about were all the interesting alternative meats; the spine-steeling offal; the briny, fresh seafood that had usually come fresh off the boat into school that same morning; the millions of sweet pastry treats; the basics of butchery; the fancy French cuisine; and the *insanely* delicious cheese, milk, cream, and butter. The day I made butter may forever be imprinted into my mind. I learned I should appreciate doing things slowly. Slow food—it's (obviously, or not so obviously) a thing. As Americans, we easily choose the drive-through on many busy weeknights because we're shuffling from job to home, to kids' activities, to church, to Zumba, and back again.

When I enrolled in the Ballymaloe Cookery School, people continuously asked, "*Ireland?* Why would you go to *Ireland* for culinary school?" Hidden in their bewildered question was the assumption that Ireland had nothing to offer the culinary scene, which is so devastatingly untrue.

First off, the grass! Ireland can grow the most luscious grass, which in turn nourishes the cows, lambs, pigs, and chickens, that then produce the richest tasting meats, eggs, cream, butter, and milk! The milk. You guys, the milk! The milk makes world-famous and irreplaceable Kerrygold butter. The city of Cork, a thirty-minute drive from BCS, once was the butter capital of the world.

Taking the course at Ballymaloe helped me gain perspective into the values I held. I began to ask myself if I could live with less—less stuff, fewer activities, less scheduled chaos. Upon arriving back in the United States, I fully realized everything we're so fortunate and blessed to possess. I have a house with so much space! Two cars in a garage full of my husband's man toys. Closets *full* of clothes, shoes, and jackets of all sorts. My kitchen. *My kitchen!* My kitchen with a dishwasher, big sink, blender, stove, gadgets of *all kinds*, and food. My kids have neighborhood friends and a school for learning. We belong to a brilliant church community. The farmers' market in my community is vibrant and thriving.

On that first day back at home, after the life-changing experience of Ballymaloe, I stood behind my own kitchen counter, whipping up some Christmas treats. All I could think about were the beautiful people I had been surrounded by over the past twelve weeks. And everything was *grand*, as they say in Ireland: It's *grand!*

Being around expats and international travelers is energizing, challenging, confusing, fun, and silly. Our lodging in Ireland was a challenge to live in, which taught me to alter my approach and my point of view, and for that, I'm thankful. Darina Allen, owner of BCS and basically the Julia Child of Ireland, and everyone at the school inspired me to believe I can do anything. My world became bigger by traveling to the quiet countryside of Shanagarry. At Ballymaloe we never said "Goodbye"; we only bid each other "Cheerio, until we see you again next time."

Once my moment in time at Ballymaloe had passed, I ended up working in two roles in the US that were valuable to my future but weren't, at the time, exactly what I had hoped for. First, a year in a catering position at a large grocery store chain. Kale salad for two hundred, anyone? Next, a year working in a marketing role for a Minnesota-based, woman-owned bone broth company. Both roles taught me much, but neither was quite *my own thing.*

So, as a New Year's resolution in 2017, I formed my LLC, The Abundant Kitchen. I didn't know exactly what the business would be at that point, but I knew I loved to be in the kitchen and wanted abundance for all who were in the kitchen with me. I worked on a business plan for months: I was never going to be accused of being short on ideas! The business concept I started with was a cooking school, café, and gourmet food and kitchenware shop. I didn't know *how* I would accomplish this massive undertaking. I just knew *why*: I wanted to create a community around food, I wanted it to inspire families, and I wanted to make wholesome food more convenient.

That spring, Travis and I walked through an empty commercial storefront in the downtown area of Buffalo, Minnesota. Immediately we could see the potential. Built in the 1930s, this building had so much charm. It had big windows overlooking Buffalo Lake, a huge paver patio for alfresco dining, and a large retail space. Not only that, it had an abandoned kitchen in the back. For the past ten years, the space had been used as a purse store, and before that, it was a short-lived French restaurant. Well, the rest is history. God opened up all the doors, and, in faith, we cautiously stepped through. Then, in November of 2019, I was given the opportunity to step through a door I never dreamt of opening up—another location on Water Street in Excelsior, Minnesota. After consideration, and frankly, a gut feeling, I now have two Abundant Kitchen locations open for business.

Today, I teach cooking classes several times a week, employ several people, and host a pop-up crepe stand during the summer months. Every day I wake up wondering what fun, new person might walk through my shop door whom I might motivate to create something delicious in the kitchen. So let the recipes in this book be my invitation to you. Try them out at home, enjoy them, experiment with them, and make them your own. And if you ever find yourself in Buffalo or Excelsior, stop in and say hi. Take a cooking class. And remember to always keep your kitchen *abundant*.

Sealing a classic French paté terrine, with fluting paste,
not tinfoil at Ballymaloe Cookery School.

Wake Up!
Delightful Breakfast Foods

I find nothing more optimistic than getting into my kitchen before anyone else has stirred. I love that moment when the air is cold and still, just before it is disturbed by the whir of coffee beans. As the first and then second sip of coffee fully jolt me into awareness, I pull out eggs to bring them to room temperature and the butter to soften up. Then I search the side door of the fridge for the jelly that will top my Skillet Popover. These are my Sunday mornings. Usually, I have no idea what I'm about to make, but I turn the oven to 425°F to get the process started.

Gadget: Bench Scrape

A bench scrape is an essential kitchen gadget used in this recipe for quickly and efficiently cutting scones into triangle shapes. This handy tool is also extremely useful for cleaning up leftover dough scraps that stubbornly stick to your countertop. But a bench scrape can be used for more than bread baking—I use it to easily transfer chopped vegetables from my workbench to oven top quickly and with little mess.

Raspberry White Chocolate Scones

Yield: 8 scones

Scone making was an integral part of my experience at Ballymaloe Cookery School. On the day I was tasked with baking scones for lunch, Darina Allen walked by my station, stopped, said something to the effect of "Oh, dear, now, let me . . . uh . . . help . . . uh . . ." but instead of stopping and helping me, she carried on as quick as the lilting Irish was out of her lips, whisked away to something more important. I always wondered what she would've said had I encouraged her to teach me. As soon as I started teaching cooking classes at my kitchen store in Buffalo, requests for classes on how to bake scones came flooding in. The Ballymaloe scone recipe is the basis for my most requested rendition, which is studded with raspberries and white chocolate.

3 ¼ cups all-purpose flour

2 tablespoons granulated cane sugar

3 teaspoons baking powder

¼ teaspoon salt

6 tablespoons butter

⅓ cup white chocolate chips

½ cup raspberries

¾ cup whole milk

2 eggs

2 tablespoons Demerara sugar

1. Preheat the oven to 425°F.

2. In a large bowl, sift together the flour, granulated cane sugar, baking powder, and salt.

3. Cut the butter into cubes, toss it into the flour and work it in using your hands or a pastry blender until the butter resembles the size of peas.

4. Toss in white chocolate chips and raspberries, coating them with the flour-butter mixture. Make a well in the center.

5. In a separate small bowl, combine the wet ingredients—whisk the eggs, then add the milk, stirring thoroughly. Add egg-milk mixture to the dry ingredients and mix into a soft dough, using a Danish dough hook, if available.

6. Turn the mixture out onto a floured worktop. Knead very lightly, shaping just enough to make a round. Roll the dough out to about 1 inch thick and use a bench scrape to cut into 8 triangular scones.

7. Brush the tops with egg wash and sprinkle with crunchy Demerara or coarse granulated cane sugar. Lay at least 1 inch apart on a parchment-lined baking sheet.

8. Bake for 12–14 minutes, or until golden brown on top. Remove the scones from baking sheet and cool on a wire rack.

9. Serve split in half and slathered with double cream.

Skillet Popover

Yield: 4 servings

Oh, the memories of dining with my grandma Lorraine at the Pannekoeken Restaurant in Roseville, Minnesota. As your order was about to be delivered, waitstaff would shout across the restaurant, *"Paaanekkkkkkoekkkken!"* The idea that, in a restaurant, where it's socially acceptable to be quiet, people could freely shout across the dining room with utter abandon, and in a foreign language I didn't understand, made my eleven-year-old self want to shout back with my own free-spirited abandon.

It's easy to prepare this batter in a blender. From start to finish, this will come together fast—in about 30 minutes. Pannekoeken is perfect served with pats of butter, thick jelly, and a sprinkle of powdered sugar. Shouting is optional.

3 eggs

¾ cup half-and-half or milk

1 teaspoon almond extract

¼ teaspoon kosher salt

⅛ teaspoon freshly ground nutmeg

¾ cup flour

4 tablespoons butter, melted, cooled

1 tablespoon sunflower oil or other neutral-flavored oil

1. Preheat the oven to 425°F and place a 10-inch oven-safe skillet inside to warm. Prepare batter while the skillet preheats.

2. Combine eggs, half-and-half or milk, almond extract, kosher salt, ground nutmeg, and flour in a blender on high speed for a minute or two, until thick and creamy. With blender still running, pour in melted butter. Let batter rest on the countertop while skillet is preheating.

3. Once skillet has preheated about 10 minutes, carefully remove it from the oven and pour in the sunflower oil, giving the skillet a swirl to ensure the oil moves up the sides. Promptly pour in the batter, place the pan back into oven, and bake for 17–20 minutes, until puffy, golden, and cooked through. Serve sliced in wedges with pats of butter, marmalade, and powdered sugar. This reheats marvelously.

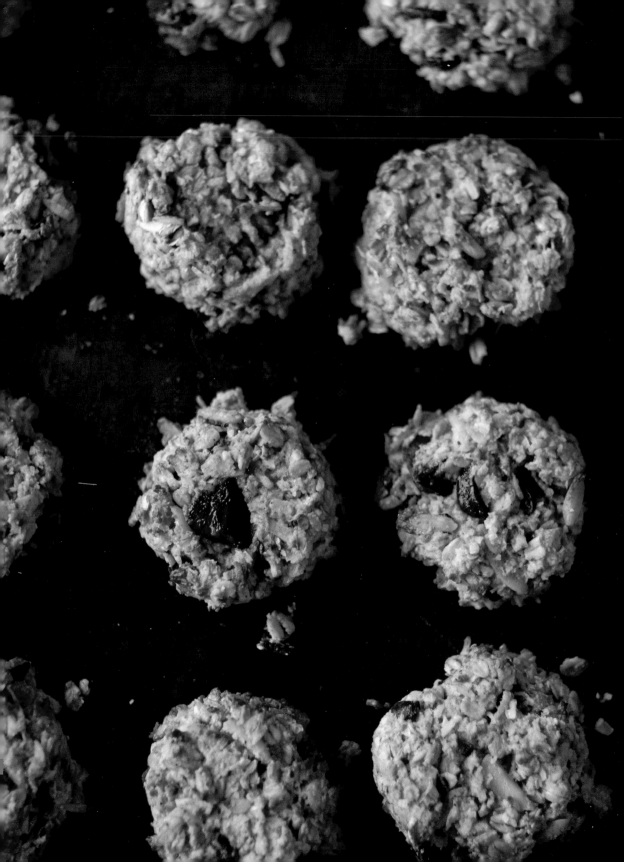

Breakfast Cookies (*Gluten-Free*)

Yield: 15 cookies

Every busy cook needs an easy breakfast cookie recipe in their recipe collection. Make these on a Sunday, and you've got quick breakfast, lunch, or snacks for the week. This recipe was originally published in Shauna Niequist's book, *Bread and Wine: A Love Letter to Life Around the Table with Recipes.* After experimenting with Shauna's version, I made a couple of small tweaks to make it my own, like adding protein powder. You can easily change the type of nut, dried fruit, or chocolate according to what you have on hand. To make these vegan, simply omit the whey protein powder.

3 large ripe bananas, can be defrosted from frozen

¼ cup oil (coconut, sunflower, or olive)

1 teaspoon almond extract

2 cups rolled oats

⅔ cup almond meal

4 tablespoons whey protein powder

⅔ cup shredded coconut

½ cup slivered almonds, toasted

¼ cup dried cherries

¼ cup dark chocolate chunks

½ teaspoon ground cinnamon

1 teaspoon baking powder

½ teaspoon kosher salt

1. Preheat oven to 350°F.

2. Combine the wet ingredients: Peel the bananas into a medium-sized bowl and mash well. Stir in oil and almond extract.

3. Combine the dry ingredients: In a separate larger bowl, combine oats, almond meal, protein powder, shredded coconut, almonds, cherries, chocolate, cinnamon, baking powder, and salt. Using a spatula, fold banana mixture into the dry ingredients. Mix well.

4. Form into cookies: Using a dry 1/4 cup measuring cup, form dough into balls and place onto a parchment-lined 10 ½ x 15 ½-inch baking sheet. Flatten tops slightly.

5. Bake for 14–16 minutes or until slightly golden around the edges. Remove from the oven, cool slightly, and transfer to a wire rack to finish cooling.

6. Store on the counter for a couple of days, but then move to the fridge to retain freshness. Keeps for 4–5 days. Can be frozen for 3–4 months.

Crepes

Yield: 4 servings

From June through September, The Abundant Kitchen operates a pop-up crepe stand on our patio that overlooks scenic Buffalo Lake. Locals usually stop at the farmers' market before wandering over for a crepe at our French bistro tables. Afterward, they usually stock up on local meats and cheeses in the store. As customers wait in line, mesmerized by the skill involved in making crepes, it seems we always hear a story or two about their first crepe, usually in Paris or travelling somewhere else far away. A crepe experience is never to be forgotten. I always rejoice when it's a customer's first crepe.

1 ½ cups all-purpose flour

2 ¼ cups whole milk

4 large eggs

¼ cup granulated cane sugar

½ teaspoon fine sea salt

1 teaspoon vanilla extract

2 tablespoons butter, melted, plus more for pan

toppings: berries, whipped cream, powdered sugar

1. Sift flour onto a piece of parchment paper, then set it aside. Whisk together milk and eggs in a large bowl. Add sugar, salt, and vanilla extract, and whisk well. Whisk in flour. Add butter and whisk well. Time allowing, let batter sit overnight in the refrigerator. Batter will perform better after resting a bit. Minimum resting time is 30 minutes.

2. Heat a small 8-inch skillet over medium-high heat. Drop in a bit of butter and let it sizzle. Drop a generous tablespoon of batter into the hot skillet, tilting the skillet to cover the base with batter.

3. After a minute, flip the crepe: First, slightly loosen the edges of the crepe, to ensure easy flipping. Next, quickly slide an offset spatula under the middle of the crepe, lift it, and flip the crepe over. Sometimes, the first crepe is your worst, but shake it off and carry on. Cook for 1 minute more. Serve with berries, whipped cream, and powdered sugar.

Gadget: Offset Spatula

The design of this handy little tool will help you easily slide under foods that are thin, like crepes. You can also use it to spread frosting across a flat surface more easily. I have two sizes in my kitchen: small and large.

Gadget: Microplane

A microplane is used for zesting citrus, freshly grating nutmeg, or finely grating Parmesan. They stay sharp forever, too. I got mine as a wedding gift fifteen years ago, and I still use the same exact one today.

Orange Ricotta Pancakes

Yield: 12 pancakes

Our most basic kids' cooking class includes this recipe for pancakes. I always have the kids sample the ricotta cheese going into the mix, which makes them frown—yet they greedily devour every morsel of pancake and beg to bring the leftovers home. There's no better way to kickstart a child's appetite than to involve them in the process of cooking. Have them crack eggs and help stir the batter for these pancakes—they'll love it!

1 ½ cups flour

3 tablespoons granulated cane sugar

1 ½ teaspoons baking powder

½ teaspoon baking soda

¼ teaspoon salt

¾ cup whole milk

¾ cup orange juice

1 egg

1 cup ricotta

½ teaspoon vanilla extract

½ teaspoon orange or lemon zest (optional)

¼ cup butter, melted, plus more for skillet in between batches of pancakes

1. In a large mixing bowl, combine flour, sugar, baking powder, baking soda, and salt with a whisk. Make a well in the center.

2. In a smaller bowl, combine milk, orange juice, egg, ricotta, vanilla extract, and zest (if using) and beat well with a whisk to combine. Pour the orange juice mixture into the well in the flour. With the whisk, start mixing in the center of the well, gradually pulling the dry ingredients into the wet. Whisk just until smooth. Pour in melted butter and mix well. Do not overmix.

3. Preheat a griddle over medium heat and grease with a tablespoon of butter. Using a scant 1/4 cup measurement, pour batter onto the hot griddle, spreading the batter slightly in the middle to ensure even cooking. Cook 2–3 minutes per side, or until deeply golden and cooked through. Serve with warm maple syrup. Leftovers can be frozen and reheated in the toaster.

Classic French Omelet

Yield: 1 omelet

Having the skill to create something as simple and elegant as a French omelet will take you very far as a host in the kitchen. One Sunday afternoon, impromptu, I invited visitors for brunch after church. Nothing was planned, nor shopped for, nor prepped. I knew, though, that I had amazing fresh eggs, cream, and herbs. I threw bacon on a sheet pan and cooked it in a 400°F oven for 20 minutes. Then I boiled water on the stove top for a batch of greens from the garden. Meanwhile, I got to cracking and whisking eggs. Everything came together in about 30 minutes. Every morsel was divine because it was quick, spanking fresh, and shared with friends.

2 really fresh eggs

2 tablespoons heavy cream

a pinch of salt

a couple of cracks black pepper

rendered pork fat or duck fat or other high-heat cooking fat

fresh herbs such as chives and Italian parsley

1. Heat a heavy-bottomed 9-inch skillet over medium-high heat. Place a dinner plate near the stove top.

2. Crack the eggs into a small bowl. Pour in the cream and season with salt and pepper. Whisk madly, as if life's chaos can be solved by whisking these eggs. (There—don't you feel at peace?)

3. Drop a dab of rendered pork fat or duck fat into the hot skillet. Tilt skillet to completely cover sides with hot fat. Once fat is sizzling, quickly pour in the whisked eggs. Pretending you have a clock on your skillet, pull eggs from 12 o'clock to the center, tilting the skillet to fill in the gap. Pull from 3 o'clock to the center, tilting and filling again. Pull from 6 o'clock to the center, tilting and filling. Lastly, pull from 9 o'clock to the center, tilting and filling the gaps. Cook for 30 seconds more. Flip the omelet edge nearest the handle onto itself, then flip again into thirds. Roll the omelet off the skillet and onto a plate. Serve with fresh herbs and kimchi.

To make for a crowd:

Set oven to 180°F. Place a large serving platter into warm oven. As the omelets finish cooking, transfer them from skillet onto the warm platter. The omelets can be left in the oven for 30 minutes. Wait to garnish with herbs until just before serving.

Sip On:
Refreshing Drinks

True hospitality always begins with offering guests something to drink. With a refreshing drink in hand, friends and family will feel welcome and at ease. My kitchen at home is set up so guests can sit around the kitchen counter and sip drinks while I cook. Or, sometimes, if the meal lends itself to it, I'll ask my guests to get in on the action. In either case, beverages are an important part of every gathering.

Thai-Basil Iced Tea

Yield: 1 large pitcher of tea

One of my childhood memories in Idaho is gazing at an enormous pitcher of water filled with tea bags and a ton of cut lemon basking in the summer heat on Aunt Lois's sunny picnic table. I specifically remember thinking how odd it was that the sun could cook the tea. But it works! This recipe uses the same tried and true method.

1 or 2 bags of black tea

a large bundle of Thai basil

a large pitcher of filtered water

Stevia or granulated cane sugar and sliced lemon, for serving

1. Place the tea bags and basil into the pitcher with the water. Set the pitcher in the afternoon sun to steep. Steeping time depends on how dark you like your tea. Four hours for medium strength, eight for strong strength.

2. After steeping, remove the tea bags and basil. Chill well. Serve over ice, sweeten if desired, and garnish with more basil and/or lemon.

A Proper Cup of Tea

Yield: 1 pot of tea (16 ounces)

The ritual of making a proper cup of tea is soothing. There's something about holding a big mug of tea cradled to my chest that feels calming. And it's most definitely warming—from the inside out!

2 teaspoons loose tea leaves, in winter

or

¼ cup fresh herbs, like mint, lemon balm, lemon verbena, and/or sweet cicely, in summer

lemon slices and honey, if desired

1. Fill a kettle or an electric teapot with fresh, cold water and bring to a boil.

2. Pour about ½ cup boiling water into your teapot and swirl the pot around to warm up the enamel. Pour that boiling water into your teacup to warm the cup.

3. Fill a small tea ball with tea leaves or fresh herbs and place it into the teapot. Pour the boiling water over the tea leaves.

4. Cover the pot and allow the leaves to steep for 3–4 minutes, depending on how strong you prefer your tea.

5. Discard warming water in the teacup, and fill it with tea. Be sure to use lots of honey if you're feeling under the weather.

Chai Tea

Yield: about 24 cups

A very spicy, fall-flavored tea, let this mixture sit overnight in the refrigerator to meld and marry before using. If you want an extra spicy mixture, heap the spices. Keeps well.

1. Place the milk in a small bowl, add spices, and mix well. Cover and refrigerate overnight. Add 1–2 teaspoons per cup of brewed chai tea.

1 can sweetened condensed milk

1 teaspoon ground cardamom

1 teaspoon ground ginger

1 teaspoon ground nutmeg

½ teaspoon ground cinnamon

½ teaspoon ground cloves

Farmers' Market Detox Drink

Yield: 1 serving

You'll probably be able to find kale, carrots, celery, honey, and herbs at your local farmers' market, but you'll need a grocery store for the lemons, limes, ginger, and cherry juice. As you drink this, chew on the mixture a bit to wake up digestion and put more pep in your step! Do not forget the ice, or the drink will taste like a garden.

Combine all ingredients in a high-powered blender or food processor and whir for 1–2 minutes, or until combined well. Serve immediately.

3 kale leaves, stemmed

½ apple, sliced

1 carrot, cut into chunks

1 stalk celery, cut into chunks

½ cup tart cherry juice or water

2 limes, juiced

1 lemon, juiced

2 tablespoons Italian parsley leaves

2 tablespoons mint leaves

a 1-inch piece of ginger

honey, to taste

4–5 ice cubes

Lunch Hour:
Soups, Sides, and Salads

Having basic cooking skills to create a homemade stock, transform that stock into a soup, bake a quick bread to accompany the soup, and compose a fresh salad with scratch vinaigrette can make the beginner cook feel like tackling more techniques in the kitchen. Don't panic; I don't mean you have to master all those skills at once! I tell my students who feel like they can't cook to focus on the basics, like the skills featured in this collection of lunch hour recipes, and then they will feel the confidence they need to move on to more advanced recipes.

Gadget: Garlic Peeler

There is nothing more agitating than trying to peel garlic that doesn't want to be peeled. If you buy farm-fresh garlic at the Minnesota Garlic Festival in Hutchinson, Minnesota, like I do every year, you know it's sticky. It's not like the garlic you get at the grocery store, which has been sitting there so long, the skin is dried out and eager to flake off. My mom bought me a garlic peeler for Christmas one year, and I haven't felt distressed while peeling garlic since!

Kale, Sausage, and Potato Soup

Yield: 4–6 servings

Everyone always loves this soup. It is comforting enough for the cold winter months, but also zippy enough for hot summer days, when the kale harvest is plentiful. Best of all, it tastes even better the next day. This is a one-pot, 30-minute meal that can work well as lunch all week long.

½ pound smoked bacon

1 pound sweet or spicy Italian sausage

1 quart water

1 ½ cups baby red potatoes, diced

1 medium onion, chopped

2 garlic cloves, minced

28 ounces chicken broth, store bought or homemade

1 15-ounce can great northern or cannellini beans

6 cups kale or other greens, coarsely chopped

1 cup heavy whipping cream

kosher salt and freshly ground black pepper, to taste

1. Place bacon in a single layer in a large stockpot over medium heat. Do not preheat pan; this helps to slowly render the fat from the bacon. Fry for about 10 minutes or until golden and crisp, stirring occasionally. Transfer the bacon to a plate lined with paper towels to drain. Chop coarsely. Drain off any additional fat from the stockpot.

2. Add the Italian sausage to the same stockpot and cook over medium-high heat until browned and cooked through, about 10 minutes. Break up the sausage into smaller pieces with a wooden spoon. Transfer the sausage to a plate lined with paper towels to drain. Note: Ground pork can be substituted here. Simply add a ½ teaspoon of freshly crushed fennel seeds, 1/4 teaspoon garlic powder, and a small pinch of red chili flakes.

3. Place the water, potatoes, onion, and garlic in the same stockpot with a pinch of salt. Cover and simmer until tender, about 10 minutes. Add the stock and meats, simmering 10 more minutes. Add beans and kale, and cook until the kale is wilted. Reduce the heat and add cream. Season with additional salt and pepper and heat through.

Potato-Leek Soup

Yield: 6 servings

Unlike in the Midwest, where soups are typically chunky, rich, and meaty, pubs in Ireland almost always feature a smooth and creamy soup without meat on the menu. The consistency of this soup is thinner than you may be used to. Served with a thick slice of brown bread and the ever-present Kerrygold butter, this soup seems as if it was meant to be dipped into by the thickly slathered brown bread.

1 large or 2 small leeks, about 3 cups, chopped

4 tablespoons butter

1 large russet potato, about 1 cup, chopped

1 medium-sized onion, about 1 cup, chopped

salt and freshly ground pepper, to taste

5 cups chicken stock

½ cup heavy whipping cream (optional)

1. Slice the dark-green tops off the leeks and set aside for stockpot (see stock recipe). Slice the light-green part of the leeks in half lengthwise. Next, slice halves into thin half-moon shapes. Plunge leek pieces into a bowl of cold water, and separate rings of leeks to remove any dirt inside the layers. Drain and set aside.

2. In a heavy-bottomed saucepan placed over medium heat, melt the butter. When it foams, add the potatoes, onions, and leeks, turning them with a spoon until well coated. Sprinkle with salt and freshly ground pepper. Cover the vegetables with a cartouche (see below) and sweat over gentle heat for 10 minutes. Add the stock.

3. Bring the vegetables and stock to a gentle boil. Simmer vegetables until soft, about 10–15 minutes.

4. Using a high-powered blender or immersion blender, puree the soup until it is smooth. Add the cream, if using. Taste for seasoning, adding more salt and pepper if desired.

What is a cartouche?

A cartouche is a cooking technique I picked up in culinary school. Basically, it's a parchment-paper lid that encourages even cooking by preventing about 20 percent less of the moisture from evaporating. This technique also helps keep moisture down around the veggies, allowing them to cook faster. I use this method to keep things moist! To make a perfectly fitting parchment-paper lid for any size saucepan, cut a piece of parchment paper as large as the top of your pan. Fold it into quarters, and then into long triangles. With the tip of the cartouche in the center of the saucepan, cut off the part of the parchment that extends beyond the sides of the pan. You should have a circle that fits perfectly in your saucepan.

Gadget: Immersion Blender

Every serious home cook should have an immersion blender for easy
pureeing of foods like soups, marinara sauce, crockpot applesauce,
vinaigrettes, or emulsions (like hollandaise), or any other instance when
you'd want to puree something but would rather not put the contents
into a blender.

The Tired Cook's Soup Stock

Yield: 6–8 quarts

Making stock is the efficient home cook's saving grace. My version is called "tired" because it uses mostly leftovers. The ingredients in soup stock are nothing I would ever add to a grocery list. Leftover bits of carrot, a head of celery about to turn, green onions or leek tops squirreled away in the freezer for stock making at a later date. And the method is perfect for the sleep-deprived working parent (kids *love* soup—especially homemade). Keep it simple. Leave the peel on that onion. Chop and drop here, folks, and move on! The best way to build up enough aromatics for a great soup stock is to keep a large bag in the deep freeze and add appropriate stock-making leftovers as you go. Parsley, thyme, rosemary, leek tops, onions, rotisserie chicken carcasses, beef bones, carrots, celery, roasted or raw garlic, lemongrass, kaffir lime leaves, and mushroom stems and caps all work great. Avoid vegetables and herbs like beets, cilantro, sage, basil, tomatoes, peppers, broccoli, cabbage, or really any cruciferous vegetable. You'll want to be sure to use a large, 10-quart stockpot for this recipe.

3 carrots

3 stalks celery

1 onion

1 head garlic

3 chicken carcasses, meat removed *or* 2 pounds of beef bones

1 large bundle Italian parsley

2–3 bay leaves

2 tablespoons kosher salt

1 tablespoon whole peppercorns

3 whole cloves

water to cover

1. Cut the carrots and celery into 3-inch chunks. Slice the onions and garlic in half, leaving the skin on. Place the chicken or beef bones, carrots, celery, onion, garlic, Italian parsley, bay leaves, salt, peppercorns, and cloves in a large stockpot. Cover with cold water. Simmer over moderate heat for about 5–6 hours. To effectively draw collagen out of the bones, keep the pot simmering at a very low bubble, not a mean boil.

2. Strain the stock into a large bowl and discard the solids. Chill the stock in the refrigerator until very cold. Skim off the fat and discard. Optional: If using chicken carcasses, the leftover fat can be used for frying. Chicken fat is also known as schmaltz. Place stock in containers, leaving about 1 inch of headroom space, then cover and freeze. The stock will keep for about 6 months in the freezer or about a week in the refrigerator.

Traditional Irish Brown Bread

Yield: 1 loaf

Found in every pub across Ireland, brown bread is an iconic part of any travel experience in Ireland. This version here comes from the Ballymaloe Cookery School. When I make this for people, they always exclaim, "Just like I had in Ireland!" The taste carries them back to a very special place and time. Use the best quality flours when making this bread. Serve at lunch or dinner with a big green salad and a bowl of soup.

1 ½ cups whole wheat flour, plus more for the baking sheet (this is the bench flour)

1 ¾ cups all-purpose flour

1 teaspoon fine salt

1 teaspoon baking soda

2 tablespoons cold butter

1 ¾ cups buttermilk

1. Preheat the oven to 375°F.

2. Mix flours, salt, and baking soda together in a large bowl. Using a pastry blender or your hands, cut in the butter until it resembles the size of peas. Make a well in the center and pour in the buttermilk. Using a Danish dough hook, stir in a full circle, starting in the center of the bowl and working toward the outside of the bowl until all the flour is incorporated. The dough should be soft but not too wet and sticky. When it all comes together, turn the dough out onto a well-floured work surface (use whole wheat flour).

3. Using your whole wheat bench flour, roll the dough around gently with floury hands for a second, just enough to tidy it up. Flip over the dough and flatten it slightly to about 2 inches. Sprinkle a little of the extra whole wheat flour onto a baking sheet. Lay the loaf on top of the flour. Using a large chef's knife, mark the surface with a deep cross and, as required to be certified as authentic Irish Brown Bread, prick in each corner to, as they say in Ireland, "let the fairies out of the bread."

4. Bake in the preheated oven for 30–40 minutes. In some ovens, it is necessary to turn the bread upside down on the baking sheet for 5–10 minutes before the end of baking to crisp up the bottom. When it is done, the bread will sound hollow when tapped. Cool on a wire rack. If you prefer a softer crust, wrapped the bread in a clean tea towel while still hot.

Gadget: Danish Dough Hook

You could use a KitchenAid mixer's dough hook—or a Danish dough hook and a little good ole elbow grease, as my grandmother might say. Use the Danish dough hook for pizza dough, scone mixes, bread doughs, or any quick bread mix. It stirs batters together quickly and with ease.

Roasted Beets

Yield: 4–6 servings

Beets are such a pain to clean and prep. But here is a recipe that will never leave you feeling the pain again!

4 medium-sized beets

1 tablespoon olive oil

salt and pepper

butter, for serving

1. Preheat the oven to 400°F.

2. Wash the beets thoroughly. Then cut off the tops and set the greens aside to make Beet-Green Sauté (see recipe). Set a large piece of parchment paper on a baking sheet.

3. Place the beets on the center of the parchment, unpeeled and whole. Drizzle them with olive oil and season with salt and pepper. Wrap the parchment around the beets, leaving enough room for the beets to steam. Place the baking sheet in the oven for 30–45 minutes, depending on size of beets.

4. To check for doneness, pierce the thickest beet with a long skewer. The skewer should go through with little resistance. If it's difficult to pierce the beet, put the pan back in the oven for another 5–10 minutes. When the beets are done, remove them from the oven and set aside until cool, about 30 minutes. When they are cool enough to handle, unwrap the beets and peel off the skin. Slice the beets and serve seasoned with butter, salt, and pepper.

Gadget: Metal Skewer

Using a metal skewer for testing doneness is more effective than a knife or fork. Not as sharp as a knife, a metal skewer guarantees you're getting an accurate read as to whether the vegetable is tender. With a longer skewer, you can pierce though larger vegetables, like roasted beets. Plus, a skewer leaves only one little hole, whereas a fork leaves four.

Beet-Green Sauté

Yield: 2 generous servings

One of my favorite cooking fats is bacon grease. Bacon grease can be heated to a moderately high heat of about 375°F, and it adds rich depth of flavor to whatever you're cooking. Collecting bacon grease is simple. After frying a batch of bacon, remove the bacon from the pan and set aside. After the grease has slightly cooled, pour it into a small glass jar. Straining the fat is optional, but I never bother—that's too much fuss. Store the jar either on the counter or refrigerate it.

1 bunch of beet greens, washed

2 tablespoons bacon grease

1 huge clove of garlic, thinly sliced

1 pinch of red chili flakes

1 tablespoon red wine vinegar

kosher salt and freshly ground black pepper

1. Remove the beets from the greens and reserve the beets for later use. Chop the beet greens into 1-inch chunks, stem and all.

2. Heat a large skillet over moderate heat, add bacon grease, and warm for 1–2 minutes. Toss in the sliced garlic and sauté gently for 2–3 minutes, or until the garlic is golden but not blackened. Add the chili flakes to the hot oil, sauté for 30 seconds, then toss in the chopped beet greens.

3. Cook until the greens reduce to about half their original size, about 8–10 minutes. Add vinegar and season with salt and pepper.

Gadget: Mandoline

A mandoline is great for consistently and thinly slicing vegetables. I use it to thinly slice brussels sprout salads, sweet potato discs, radishes for salad, or garlic for sautéing. Just watch your fingers. This is your time to practice mindfulness!

Spring Greens with Tarragon Vinegar

Yield: 1 dinner salad

1. Wash greens and pat dry with a clean tea towel.

2. Tear or chop the leaves into bite-sized pieces and scatter into a shallow bowl. Season the greens with salt and pepper. Drizzle with olive oil and vinegar.

3. Toss and garnish with edible flowers. Be happy.

2 handfuls spring greens

several cracks of freshly ground black pepper

a healthy pinch flaky sea salt

2 tablespoons good olive oil

2 tablespoons tarragon vinegar (see next recipe)

edible flowers, for garnish (optional)

CSA Veggie Storage Tips:

CSA is an abbreviation for Community Supported Agriculture. Members pay a seasonal fee to a local farmer, who then delivers a box of fresh produce to a drop site each week. Belonging to a CSA can be a great way to show your support for local farmers *and* get your fill of an abundance of fresh and sometimes unusual fruits and vegetables. If you are new to a CSA, here are some tips for CSA success! Sometimes, delivery day can be challenging, because you won't always know what will be showing up in your box.

1. Begin saving all bread bags, apple bags, lemon bags, and bags of all kinds and reuse them for the produce, which will be mostly loose. You'll want to keep your refrigerator organized, because keeping the produce in order leads to easier weeknight meal planning.

2. Prepare to eat a lot of greens. Did I say *a lot*? I meant it.

3. Bookmark interesting recipes you always wanted to try but never really had a reason to prepare. Now you will need that random recipe for pea shoots—get ready to be adventurous in the kitchen!

4. Know that there's always a possibility of finding a green caterpillar or other bug in your produce. Don't worry. This is organic produce—remember, bugs mean no pesticides. Just toss them into the garbage and continue on.

5. Keep moisture-loving veggies, like radishes, in a tightly sealed baggie with a slightly damp paper towel.

Tarragon Vinegar

I so hope you are a fan of tarragon. The fragrance, with hints of
licorice and anise, is very unique. There's really no recipe! Just
place a handful of tarragon in a pint-sized glass jar. Pour white
wine vinegar over the tarragon. Steep for a week then store in
the refrigerator indefinitely. To use, mix with olive oil to make a
vinaigrette or with mayo to make a creamy dressing. If you have
a dehydrator, it's very easy to make your own dried tarragon to
use throughout the year. Simply place the clipped tarragon, still
on the stalk, in a single layer on the dehydrator shelves. Place
the dryer on low heat and run for 2-3 days, or until nice and
crispy to the touch. Run your fingers down the stalk to loosen
the leaves, and then store in an airtight container indefinitely.
I use the tarragon in a mayo-vinegar salad dressing that tastes
great over cucumbers.

Winter Salad

Yield: 4 side salads

Minnesota vegetable and produce growers have developed farming practices that allow them to extend their growing season much longer. Hoop houses grow greens well into the colder months, even in the dead of winter. Finding a local farmer to provide you with tender young greens for this salad should be easier than ever. Carrots can be stored well into winter and even acquire a sweeter flavor as sugars start to develop while they are stored.

My favorite part of this salad is the varying textures and flavors. Don't be afraid to substitute these suggested ingredients for what you have on hand. The colorful carrot, shredded on a box grater, for more sweetness. The pungent green onion. The sweetness of the apple or pear. Saltiness from the cheese. And, the simplicity of the dressing. Amen.

4 heaping cups tender young greens, chopped

2 large carrots, grated (about 1 cup)

3 green onions, sliced (about ½ cup)

1 small apple or pear, diced (about 1 cup)

1 cup mild cheese, diced (such as Sunnyside Creamery cheddar, Jarlsberg, or Swiss)

⅓ cup sunflower seeds

½ cup dried fruit (cranberries, blueberries, golden raisins, etc.)

1 lemon, juiced (about 3 tablespoons juice)

3 tablespoons olive oil

gray sea salt and freshly ground black pepper, to taste

1. In a large salad bowl or on four individual salad plates, arrange the greens as a beautiful bed for the rest of the vegetables.

2. Scatter the grated carrot, sliced green onions, chopped apple or pear, diced cheese, sunflower seeds, and dried fruit atop the greens.

3. Squeeze the lemon over the greens. Drizzle with olive oil. Season with a pinch of sea salt and freshly ground black pepper. Feel healthy.

Gadget: Cheese Knife

Until I had a kitchen store, I didn't even know the cheese knife existed. Several customers came in asking if I carried the mystical "cheese knife." Well, with a little persistence, I found the wholesaler, and now no cheese can stand my slicing prowess! This thing slices through soft cheese, hard cheese, or anything sticky, like a Brie.

Wild Mushrooms in Sherry-Cream Sauce

1. Fill the kitchen sink with water and add mushrooms. Swish around and let sit for 10 minutes or so, allowing the critters to crawl out of the insides. Swish around a bit more, then move to a kitchen towel, further inspecting for critters. Slice mushrooms in half and give them another bath if the insides look like they just came in from the wilderness, i.e., dirty and full of bugs (you are forewarned).

2. Heat olive oil and butter in a large (preferably cast-iron) skillet over moderate heat until sizzling. Toss in cleaned wild mushrooms and cook for about 10–15 minutes, stirring frequently. Cooking wild mushrooms to a beautiful caramelization takes a lot longer than cooking store-bought mushrooms because of the higher moisture content. Wild mushrooms will release a lot of water, and at one point you'll most likely have a soupy mess, but continue cooking and be patient. Turn up the heat a little if you're getting antsy.

3. Once the wild mushrooms have begun to brown and have shrunk to about half their size, and you've cooked down any water they've released, season with salt and pepper, stir in garlic and thyme, and sauté for 1–2 minutes more. Deglaze with sherry and cook until reduced by half. Stir in cream and bring up to a gentle bubble. Scatter ramps over the mushrooms and season with additional salt and pepper. Serve with baked potato or pasta.

1 pound wild mushrooms

3 tablespoons olive oil

2 tablespoons butter

kosher salt and freshly ground black pepper

2 cloves garlic, minced

1 teaspoon fresh thyme, minced

½ cup very dry sherry wine

3 tablespoons heavy cream

¼ cup ramps, chives, or green onions, finely minced

Foraging 101: A Beginner's Guide to Finding Morel Mushrooms in the Wild

Being in the wilderness is something that clears the mind and refreshes the soul. If while hunting for the illusive morel, you're skunked, at least you will feel renewed by a stint of vigorous walking in the fresh air. Morels are known to grow all over the United States, on the East Coast, in Vermont, in central Georgia, in the Midwest, and farther west into Oklahoma. The Pacific Northwest can be a rich place to find morels, too. A combination of the time of year they're in season, the color and texture of the mushrooms, and just the right amount of moisture in the woods in which they grow all contribute to the morel's reputation of being notoriously challenging to discover. With this guide, I hope you'll be encouraged to get out into the woods and give it a try.

Morels are in season when:

- the lilacs and cherry blossoms are in bloom.
- the temperature at night doesn't drop below 60°F.
- there's no frost on your windows in the morning.
- it has rained a lot and remained humid.

Look for morels:

- when you gaze into the treetops. You can easily decipher the dead trees from the leafed out trees. Go to the base of dead trees.
- on mossy slopes below dead trees. Some say Elm trees, but I think any dead wood is a place to look.
- where ramps, jack-in-the-pulpit, and other wildflowers grow.
- in low lying, moist areas. You should see the ground covered in moss and 3–4 inches of grassy, patchy undergrowth.

Walk slow, stop, and look around!

- As you walk through the woods, walk slow, stop occasionally, and slowly glance at the ground all around you. This may help you spot a hiding mushroom more easily!
- When you pick a morel, remember to leave the roots for next year's crop. Using a small paring knife, slice the mushroom at the base.

Dress properly:

- Wear rubber boots for mucking through swamps, dark-colored clothing that covers all your skin, a hat, and bug spray to repel wood ticks—are all required.
- As you are walking through the woods, occasionally glance down at your pant legs in search of wood ticks. Check your friend's back, too!
- Checking for wood ticks after being in the woods is a must. When you come in from the woods, take your clothes off outside, shake them out, shake out your hair, and check your hairline and behind your ears, then head for the shower and wash off.

Forage for other wild things, such as:

- ramps, fiddlehead ferns, asparagus, sorrels, dandelion greens, and chicken of the woods mushrooms.

Know a false morel and other inedible mushrooms:

- A false morel has a cap unlike a morel—the stem grows up into the cap and is connected differently than on a morel.
- Consult a guidebook to identify edible and inedible mushrooms. I recommend the *National Audubon Society Field Guide to North American Mushrooms.*

Hearty Main Dishes:
Quick Dinners

Having been fortunate enough to stay at home with Christian and Liam until they were preschool-age made me appreciate how challenging and lonely being a stay-at-home mom can be. In between the constant unknowns of motherhood—*Would they spike a fever today? Would they have poopy, messy blowouts? Would they take the beloved two-hour nap?*—was the reassurance that I could cook. I could cook, create, and be in the kitchen with certainty. When the boys got a little bit older, and I started working full-time, I experienced the other side of the time crunch most parents find themselves in. I realized getting wholesome food on the table was a constant challenge. And that's where the mission for The Abundant Kitchen was born: providing a blueprint for wholesome food with convenience. This collection of dinner recipes is meant to be convenient food, with a wholesome, comfort food flavor. Enjoy.

Gadget: Herb Stripper

This simple gadget allows you to quickly remove the leaves from woody herbs like thyme, oregano, and rosemary.

Chicken and Dumplings

Yield: 4 generous servings

Chicken and dumplings is something you may crave on a blustery winter day. Comfort food. I love making this for my family, as it reminds me of my childhood Betty Crocker cookbook. This recipe comes together in a snap if you keep a couple of pantry staples on hand: frozen mixed vegetables, stock, onion, milk, and shredded chicken. Enjoy.

3 tablespoons butter

1 medium onion, chopped

2 teaspoons fresh thyme, minced

kosher salt and freshly ground black pepper, to taste

3 tablespoons all-purpose flour

4 cups chicken stock

2 cups cooked chicken, shredded

2 cups frozen mixed vegetables

1 cup milk or cream

1. Melt butter in a 4-quart saucepan over medium heat. Add onion and cook until softened, or about 8 minutes. Stir in thyme, and salt and pepper to taste. Add flour and cook for 3–4 minutes, stirring frequently. Slowly whisk in stock to make a thick gravy. Boil until slightly thickened over medium-high heat, about 10 minutes.

2. Add chicken and frozen vegetables, simmering for about 5 minutes to blend flavors. Remove from heat and add milk. Season with additional salt and pepper to taste. Return to heat and add dumpling dough (see below). Cover and gently simmer over medium-high heat for 6–8 minutes, or until a toothpick inserted into the center of a dumpling comes out clean. Serve.

Dumplings

Yield: 5–7 dumplings

1. In a small bowl, use a whisk to thoroughly combine the flour, baking powder, and salt. Cut in the lard or butter with a fork or pastry cutter. Stir in the egg, milk, and parsley. Drop by tablespoon into hot, simmering stew.

1 cup all-purpose flour

1 teaspoon baking powder

½ teaspoon kosher salt

⅛ cup lard or butter

1 egg

⅓ cup milk

1 teaspoon fresh Italian parsley, chopped

Almond-Parmesan-Crusted Walleye with Tartar Sauce

Yield: 4 fillets

Could there be any other dish more Midwestern than a good, crispy filet of walleye? Walleye is an elusive species to even the most skilled angler. When properly prepared, the flesh should be flaky and fresh tasting, with a good coating of crisp, well-seasoned bread crumbs on the outside. When Travis and I were pregnant with our first child, we moved from the Twin Cities to small, charming Buffalo, hoping to re-create memories of our own rural upbringings for our growing family. We bought a home overlooking Lake Pulaski, where Travis fished for walleye in his Lund fishing boat. This recipe became my favorite way to prepare walleye. Don't substitute the panko or almond meal—both are key to the crispy outside!

4 walleye fillets

¼ teaspoon kosher salt

⅛ teaspoon freshly ground black pepper

1 cup flour

2 eggs

¾ cup panko crumbs

¼ cup almond meal

½ cup Parmesan cheese

1 tablespoon Italian herbs

1 tablespoon butter

2 tablespoons olive oil

2 fresh lemons cut into wedges, for serving

1. Season both sides of the walleye fillets with salt and pepper. Set up your breading station: Using three shallow dishes, place the flour in one dish, the eggs in the second dish, and the panko, almond meal, Parmesan, and Italian herbs in the third dish. Whisk the eggs and give the almond-Parmesan mixture a good stir.

2. Carefully dip both sides of the seasoned fillets into the flour, and then into the egg, and then into almond-Parmesan mixture, pressing the almond-Parmesan mixture into the fish. Once fillet is well coated, set aside and continue dipping the other fillets. Once all the fillets are coated, press any leftover crumbs into the fish.

3. Preheat a large, deep cast-iron skillet over medium-high heat for a few minutes. Once skillet is hot, pour in the oil and butter. When the fat has stopped bubbling and hissing and is shimmering, add the fish. Fry over moderate heat until deep golden brown, for about 5–6 minutes. Flip and continue to cook until deep golden brown and cooked through, about 5–6 more minutes. Move to a 200°F oven until ready to serve. Serve with freshly squeezed lemon wedge and tartar sauce (see next page).

Gadget: Fish Spatula

The fish spatula is a must for every kitchen. Its thin blade construction makes sliding under eggs, burgers, or anything you need to flip with agility a breeze. Because the blade is serrated, oil drains quickly, too.

Tartar Sauce

Yield: 1 ½ cups sauce

1. In a small bowl, gently stir together mayonnaise, lemon juice, pickle, pickle juice, Tabasco, salt, and pepper. Taste for seasonings. Serve immediately or refrigerate until ready to serve.

1 cup real mayonnaise

1 tablespoon lemon juice, freshly squeezed

1 medium-sized gherkin pickle, diced finely (about a tablespoon)

1 teaspoon pickle juice

2 shakes of Tabasco

⅛ teaspoon salt

⅛ teaspoon freshly ground pepper

Grilled Pheasant Breast

Yield: 2 servings

Brining wild game and using caul fat are two tricks I've learned to prepare many scrumptious game meals. Brining is the simple method of infusing meat fibers with salt molecules. It makes the meat more tender and juicy. Don't skip this step! You can also brine chicken, turkey, and pork.

The caul fat is something most butchers probably toss. Ask your butcher, after their next hog slaughter, for a package of caul fat. One hog will provide you with enough caul fat for about four times this recipe. Caul fat is a thin, lacelike membrane found in animals like cows, sheep, and pigs (shown on next page). The pig caul fat is the best. I use it as a wrapping for meats with less fat marbling, like pheasant. Caul fat lends a juiciness, kind of like wrapping in bacon.

8 tablespoons kosher salt, plus more
    for seasoning

2 quarts cold water

4 boneless pheasant breasts

4 pieces of caul fat measuring
    6 x 6 inches

freshly ground black pepper

high-heat cooking oil, like sunflower oil

Directions on following page

1. In a large bowl, combine the salt and water, stirring until dissolved. Place the pheasant breasts into the brine mixture for a minimum of 30 minutes and up to 12 hours. Refrigerate the pheasant if you plan to brine for more than 1 hour.

2. Remove the meat from the brine mixture and blot off excess water using a clean dish towel or paper towels. Lay out sheets of caul fat on a clean work surface. Season the pheasant breast with a pinch of kosher salt and a couple of cracks of freshly ground black pepper. Place the pheasant breasts in the center of the caul fat and loosely wrap caul fat around each breast, making a meat parcel.

3. Preheat the grill for 10–15 minutes. If you are using an indoor grill pan, preheat pan for 2–4 minutes, or until smoking hot. Clean grill grates and lightly oil.

4. Grill pheasant 6–8 minutes per side, or until until cooked through.

5. Slice the meat on the bias and serve with crusty bread and green lentils.

Oven-Baked Salmon with Kale Cream Sauce

Yield: 4 servings

Travis's birthday in August signals that summer is coming to a close. To squeeze every last drop from the season, we head east to Door County, Wisconsin, where we charter a boat in the cold waters of Lake Michigan for what Travis calls "a shopping trip." We love bringing home the best fresh salmon that's frozen right on the dock. On cold winter nights, I make this recipe as a reminder of summer. To make this meal come together quickly, I like to draw from my bags of blanched kale in the freezer, which I squirrel away just for this sauce. Baking the fish en papillote, or in a paper wrapper, keeps steam inside the parcel, creating a juicy, moist fish. Be sure to keep the parchment paper somewhat loose around the fish to create a little steam pocket.

2 pounds salmon filet

salt and freshly ground black pepper

2–4 tablespoons butter

sprig of dill or fennel (optional)

1. Preheat oven to 375°F.

2. Pat the salmon filet dry with paper towels. Season with salt and pepper. Put a smear of butter and a sprig of fennel or dill (or leave herbs out all together) on top of the salmon filet, smear a little butter in the center of a large sheet of parchment paper, place the salmon on top, and fold the parcel so that the ends meet, crimping the edges shut, either by folding or by stapling (but don't lose those staples!). Seal and crimp well to make sure that none of the juices escape. Place on a baking sheet and bake 15–20 minutes.

3. Plate the fish onto a serving dish. Spoon the Kale Cream Sauce (see below) over the fish and serve immediately.

Kale Cream Sauce

Yield: 4 servings

1. Remove the stems from the kale, then roughly chop and cook the leaves in 2 cups of boiling, salted water. Cook for 4–5 minutes or until soft. Drain, press out all the water, and chop finely (or pulse in a food processor until minced).

1 cup curly kale

½ cup heavy cream

6 tablespoons butter, cubed

2. Pour the cream into a small saucepan and simmer over low heat until reduced to about 3 tablespoons. Then, over very low heat, whisk in the butter bit by bit. Stir in the kale.

Dutch-Oven-Roasted Tarragon Chicken with Tallow-Roasted Potatoes

Yield: 6–8 servings

Every cook should have a basic roast chicken recipe to rely on. This version is founded on Darina Allen's recipe from Ballymaloe. I've made a couple of my own substitutions. Sometimes, I use the rosemary that grows in my sunny dining room window all winter long.

1 whole chicken weighing about 3 ½ pounds

salt and freshly ground black pepper

1 sprig of tarragon plus 1 tablespoon tarragon, chopped

2 tablespoons butter, softened

1. Preheat the oven to 375°F.

2. Season the cavity of the chicken with a pinch of salt and a couple of cracks of black pepper. Stuff a sprig of tarragon inside.

3. Warm a Dutch oven with a tight-fitting lid on the stove top over medium heat.

4. Mix the remaining chopped tarragon with the softened butter. Smear half the butter-tarragon mixture over chicken breasts, then season chicken with a pinch of salt and pepper. Turn the chicken, breast side down, into the preheated Dutch oven and gently fry it until the chicken is light golden brown, about 3–4 minutes.

5. Meanwhile, smear the remaining butter-tarragon mixture over the backside of the chicken and season with more salt and pepper as it fries. When the breasts have browned, flip the chicken over, place the lid on Dutch oven and move it to the preheated oven. Bake for 1 ½ hours.

6. To test for doneness, wiggle the leg a bit—it should want to easily separate from the body. Additionally, pierce the chicken between the breast and thigh; the juices should run clear with no trace of pink. Transfer the chicken to a carving board and allow to rest for a minimum of 10–15 minutes before carving.

Tallow-Roasted Potatoes *(Recipe Next Page)*

Tallow-Roasted Potatoes

1 pound potatoes

2 tablespoons tallow, melted*

2 cloves of garlic, whole, peeled

2 teaspoons fresh rosemary, minced

salt and freshly ground black pepper

truffle salt, for finishing

Yield: 4 side servings

1. Preheat oven to 400°F.

2. For a crispier roast potato, peel off the skin. For a chewier potato, leave the skin on.

3. Slice the potatoes into wedges and arrange evenly on a parchment-lined baking sheet.

4. In a small saucepan, melt the tallow. Add garlic, minced rosemary, salt, and pepper. Drizzle over the potatoes and stir to coat evenly.

5. Place the baking sheet in the oven and bake for 20 minutes. Once the potatoes begin to caramelize, flip them over. Bake for an additional 10–20 minutes, or until they can be pierced easily with a skewer and are a deep golden brown.

6. Finish with a sprinkling of truffle salt.

* Ask for tallow at your local butcher shop, or, if you're ambitious and curious, make your own. See the recipe on page 89.

Gadget: Dutch Oven

Having a high-quality Dutch oven in the kitchen is a must for making big pots of soup, roast chickens, wild game roasts, and bread boules! The heavy construction retains heat very well. These vessels can be passed down to the next generation of serious cooks.

Mediterranean Lamb Skewers with Chimichurri and Cucumber-Herb Yogurt Sauce

Yield: 8 skewers

The components of this meal can successfully stand alone, but when prepared together, you've got a feast fit for a king! Be sure to follow the technique of grating onion over the meat—it makes the meat so flavorful. Also try boiling rice (see below). If you've ever failed at making rice (think: pots with rice stuck on the bottom forever; lid lifting gone bad, rice with enough leftover water you could swim in it; or hard-as-nails, crispy rice), here is your no-fail rice-preparation method to forever end all rice failures.

2 pounds ground lamb

½ onion

2 tablespoons curry powder

kosher salt and freshly ground black pepper

Olive oil, for grilling

1. Place ground lamb in a large mixing bowl. Using a box grater, grate onion over the lamb so the onion juices drip onto the lamb.

2. Season with curry powder, salt, and pepper. Using your hands, combine well but don't overmix.

3. Form ½-cup portions of the lamb into long hot dog shapes and thread a skewer through the center. Heat up your grill. To prevent sticking on the grill, mist the lamb with olive oil.

4. When the grill is nice and hot, place skewers on grill. Cook on each side for 7–9 minutes, or until cooked through. Serve with Chimichurri and Cucumber-Herb Yogurt Sauce.

Cucumber-Herb Yogurt Sauce

Yield: 1 ½ cups sauce

1. Combine all the ingredients in a small bowl and mix well. Serve immediately or refrigerate for up to 3 days. Flavor gets better with time.

1 cup Greek yogurt

1 cup peeled, seeded, and finely chopped cucumber

2 tablespoons onion, finely minced

1 small garlic clove, finely minced

Juice of 1 lemon, about 4 tablespoons

3 tablespoons milk (more to achieve desired consistency)

½ cup assorted herbs (such as dill, mint, Italian parsley, and oregano), finely chopped

½ teaspoon kosher salt

⅛ teaspoon white pepper

Gadget: Extra-Virgin Olive Oil (EVOO) Sprayer

My EVOO sprayer was a gift many years ago from my gadget-savvy mother-in-law. Use it just like you would use a nonstick cooking spray, but without any of the nasty chemical propellants. I've had mine for years, and it has never clogged.

Chimichurri

Yield: 4 servings

1. Using a high-powered blender or large food processor with the motor running on high, process the garlic clove until finely minced.

2. Add the remaining ingredients. Pulse until combined. Let sit at room temperature for 1 hour before serving to allow the flavors to bloom.

1 clove garlic, peeled

1 cup Italian parsley leaves

1 cup cilantro leaves

1 cup mint leaves

2 tablespoons oregano leaves

$\frac{1}{3}$ cup water

3 tablespoons white wine vinegar

$\frac{1}{3}$ cup olive oil

1–2 teaspoons red chili flakes

$\frac{1}{4}$ teaspoon kosher salt

$\frac{1}{8}$ teaspoon black pepper

Boiled Rice

Yield: 6–8 servings

Think of this rice method as you would boiling a pot of pasta noodles. A big kettle of water is put to the boil, then the rice is poured in all at once and boiled until al dente, or firm to the bite. The end result is like a pilaf. This is a terrific method for entertaining because the rice will hold in a low oven for up to 2 hours prior to serving.

3–4 quarts of water

1 tablespoon salt

2 cups long grain rice, like basmati or jasmine

butter, for buttering dish plus more for rice (about 2 tablespoons)

1. Preheat oven to 350°F.

2. Heat a large kettle of water over high heat until it boils.

3. Add the salt and the rice to boiling water and bring back up to a boil. Boil rice 5–8 minutes, or until al dente.

4. Drain the rice in a colander. Then pour the rice into a 13 x 9-inch buttered casserole dish, dot the top with butter, cover with foil, and bake for 15 minutes. Fluff and serve.

One-Pot Lasagna

Yield: 4 - 6 servings

As a cooking class instructor, I have my finger on the pulse of customer-requested cooking techniques, and recipes for one-pot meals are something I'm asked for time and time again. And why not? Fewer dishes make prep and cleanup fast and easy. This recipe is cheesy and satisfying. My use of dried herbs here is intended to help encourage the younger palates to enjoy what I call "real food."

1 pound ground beef

½ large onion, chopped

1 clove garlic, minced

24 ounces tomato sauce (see next recipe)

16 ounces cottage cheese

10 lasagna noodles

2 ½ cups chopped tomatoes (canned works too)

1 tablespoon dried parsley

1 heaping teaspoon dried basil

kosher salt and freshly ground black pepper, to taste

scant ½ cup water

1 ½ cups mozzarella cheese, shredded

1. Working in a deep 10-inch skillet with a tight-fitting lid, brown beef until cooked through.

2. Add onion and season with salt and pepper. Sauté until the onion is soft and translucent. Stir in the garlic.

3. Pour half the tomato sauce over the beef. Layer all the cottage cheese over the sauce.

4. Break up half the lasagna noodles so they fit into the pan—it's okay if they overlap a bit.

5. Add the remaining tomato sauce, tomatoes, dried herbs, salt, and pepper.

6. Layer the remaining lasagna noodles, breaking them apart as needed. Pour the water over the noodles, cover, and simmer over medium heat for 25–30 minutes, reducing heat about halfway through cooking time.

7. Once noodles are tender, top with mozzarella, cover, and cook until melted, about 3–5 minutes. Serve with hunks of bread and a crisp salad.

Charred Tomato Sauce with Fennel

Yield: 24–32 ounces (depending on size of tomatoes)

The fennel here is the "top secret" special ingredient. Don't skip it. My preference is to make this sauce at the height of summer produce, when tomatoes beg for delicious application and are being dropped at your front doorstep by neighbors with abundant gardens. Look at your local farmers' market for what are called "paste" tomatoes. They have less juice and are good to make into a thick, rich sauce. The end result is a thick tomato sauce. (My sister says this sauce is "totally drinkable.") Use on top of zoodles (zucchini noodles) with loads of Parmesan, on eggplant or chicken Parmesan, as pizza sauce, or as dip for mozzarella sticks. If turning on your oven midsummer makes you sweat just thinking about it, go ahead and try aluminum roasting tins on the outdoor grill. It works beautifully. Cleanup is a breeze. The recipe and cooking time are the same.

6–8 tomatoes, cut into 1-inch chunks

2–4 whole, peeled cloves garlic

1 large sprig oregano, about 1 tablespoon, stem removed

½ large red onion, cut into 1-inch chunks

1 large carrot, cut into 1-inch chunks

2 teaspoons fennel seed

6 tablespoons olive oil

2 teaspoons salt

½ teaspoon pepper

½ cup fresh basil, stems removed

¾ cup Parmesan cheese, grated

1. Preheat oven to 400°F. Evenly distribute tomatoes, garlic, oregano, onion, carrot, and fennel on a large baking sheet. Drizzle with olive oil. Add salt and pepper. Toss to combine and coat vegetables well.

2. Roast in oven for about 15–20 minutes, checking at the 15-minute mark. When vegetables start to caramelize and the edges turn slightly black, remove from oven. Let cool slightly.

3. Place grilled tomato mixture in a blender or food processor; let steam escape through feed chute. Process until smooth. Add basil and Parmesan cheese. Run on high speed until well combined. Use immediately or chill well, and then place into freezer-safe containers and freeze for up to one year.

Taco Meat

Yield: 12 servings

1. Heat a large skillet over moderate heat. Add ground beef and cook through, breaking it up as it cooks but not moving it around too much. Ideally, the meat will caramelize after about 8–10 minutes.

2. Once the meat is almost cooked through, add the vegetables and sauté for 3–4 minutes.

3. Add garlic and give the pan a stir, then add the tomato paste and cook for another minute.

4. Sprinkle in the spices and mix to combine well. Pour in the stock or water and bring to a gentle simmer for 5–7 minutes. Serve in hard or soft taco shells with shredded cheese, shredded lettuce, black olives, pickled jalapeños, diced tomato, and sour cream, if desired.

1 ½ pounds ground beef

½ large onion, chopped

1 giant carrot or 2 small, grated

2 cloves garlic, minced

¼ cup tomato paste

2 teaspoons kosher salt

1 teaspoon freshly ground black pepper

2 tablespoons ground cumin

1–2 tablespoons chili powder

1 tablespoon smoked paprika

1 teaspoon dried oregano

1 pinch cinnamon

1 cup chicken stock or water

taco shells, hard or soft

taco toppings such as shredded cheese, lettuce, black olives, pickled jalapeños, diced tomato, salsa, and sour cream

Homemade Salsa, or Summer in a Jar

Yield: 12 pints

1. Place all ingredients in a stainless-steel or ceramic-coated kettle and bring to a boil. Simmer for 30 minutes, stirring occasionally.

2. Meanwhile, prepare jars and boiled lids by running them through the dishwasher. Have them good and hot when it's time to pour in the ingredients.

3. Bring a large, deep covered kettle of water to a rolling boil on the stove top.

4. When salsa is done simmering, ladle it through a wide funnel into the hot jars, leaving ½ inch of headspace. *Important*: Place caps on the jars and slightly tighten the lids—leave lids loose to relieve pressure in the jars and avoid breaking any jars in your water bath.

- 10 cups chopped tomatoes (about 25–30 tomatoes)
- 5 cups chopped onion (about 6–8 medium onions)
- 2 cups chopped, seeded bell peppers (about 3 large peppers)
- 4 cups chopped, seeded hot chili peppers—jalapeño (7–9), Hungarian wax (4–6)
- 3–4 large cloves peeled, crushed garlic
- 1 large bundle of cilantro, chopped
- 1 heaping tablespoon kosher salt
- ¾ cup freshly squeezed lime juice
- ¾ cup apple cider vinegar

5. Place a rack or towel in the bottom of your water bath. Use a jar lifter to lower jars into the boiling water, and boil for 30 minutes. Remove jars with your jar lifter, place on a towel-lined countertop, and allow them to come to room temperature.

6. Listen for popping or sealing noises coming from the jars—this is a sign that the jars are sealing properly. When the jars are cool, test the seal by pressing down on the lids. If a lid can be pressed down or makes a popping sound, the jar is not properly sealed. Place this jar in the refrigerator and consume within two weeks. Sealed jars can be stored at room temperature in a cool, dark place for up to one year.

Important Canning Tips

Canning is a great way to preserve the harvest, but it's so important to follow a few simple food safety rules. Here are a few *really important* canning tips my mama taught me:

1. *Do not* tighten your caps—give them one or two loose turns onto the jar. If lids are too tight, pressure will build in the jar and it may break. Believe me, I've experienced salsa in a boiling-hot water bath firsthand.

2. *Everything* must be treated in hot water to prevent the growth of bacteria. Caps (plunge in boiling-hot water), jars (run them through the dishwasher right before you are ready to use them), ingredients (bring to a boil)—all *hot as Hades*. You get the picture.

3. Use a rack in the bottom of the hot water bath, or, as my mom and I do, use a simple kitchen towel. Place a kitchen towel in the bottom of the water bath, place jars on top.

4. Caps and jars should be pristinely clean to prevent bacteria growth and ensure a nice seal when the jars come out of the hot water bath.

5. One tool you *cannot* live without while canning is a jar lifter. A funnel is useful and makes the process a little cleaner, but it's not absolutely necessary.

6. Wear latex gloves while chopping to avoid transferring the spice of peppers or garlic to your eyes later on.

7. Remember why you are sweating it out—to provide a healthier future for the people you love.

Sweet Indulgences:
Dessert

I come from a family that shared dessert at the end of our meals more often than not: Waldorf salad, seven-layer bars, pumpkin pie, or Jell-O instant pudding. As kids, we were tasked with vigorously shaking the mason jar until the thin milk turned to pudding. Now as a mom myself, I see this as a successful ploy to keep the kids busy!

Quick and Easy Raspberry Brûlée

Yield: 8 servings

Berry season in Minnesota is both fleeting and treasured. To maximize these coveted gems of flavor, I prefer a preparation method that requires little fuss, like this method.

1 ¼ cups heavy cream

¾ cup powdered sugar

2 ½ pints fresh raspberries

⅓ cup turbinado sugar

1. Using a stand-up mixer fitted with the whisk attachment (or a handheld mixer), beat the cold cream until soft peaks form. Add the powdered sugar and combine well.

2. Using a spatula, gently fold in the raspberries. Don't worry if some break up; it's still going to taste fabulous.

3. Pour the mixture into a large 2 ½-quart serving dish and top with the turbinado sugar.

4. Meanwhile, heat up the broiler.

5. Place the dish directly under the hot broiler and watch carefully for about 5 minutes. Do not walk away from the oven—open the door and check on the dish several times. Just when you begin to see little blackened spots on the surface of the whipped cream, remove the dish from the oven. Place the dessert into the refrigerator to allow the topping to harden. This should take anywhere from 15 minutes to several hours.

Rosemary Roll-and-Slice Shortbread

Yield: about 2 dozen

This is a great recipe to have in the freezer for unexpected company or if you just want to bake a couple of cookies at a time. The dough is frozen until ready to use. How thick or thin you slice them is up to you. Do you prefer a crisper cookie? Slice ¼-inch thick. I like mine a little thicker, about ½-inch thick. The thicker cut makes them a teensy bit doughy in the middle and less crispy.

1 cup (2 sticks) butter, softened

¾ cup granulated cane sugar

1 large egg

1 teaspoon vanilla extract

2 ½ cups sifted all-purpose flour

3 tablespoons chopped fresh rosemary

¾ teaspoon salt

½ cup turbinado sugar

1. Place the softened butter into the bowl of a stand-up mixer and beat on medium speed for 2 minutes.

2. Add the sugar and mix on medium speed until light and fluffy, about 2 minutes. Mix in the egg and vanilla.

3. Add the sifted flour, chopped rosemary, and salt, mixing on low speed until incorporated.

4. Divide the dough in half and shape each piece into a log. Place each log on a 12 x 6-inch sheet of parchment paper. Roll the dough in parchment to 1 ½ inches in diameter, pressing a ruler along the edge of the parchment at each turn to narrow the log and force out the air. Transfer the logs rolled in parchment to the freezer. Freeze for 1 hour or up to 6 months.

5. Preheat the oven to 375°F. Line a baking sheet with a fresh sheet of parchment paper.

6. Remove parchment from the outside of the logs.

7. Sprinkle the turbinado sugar on a cookie sheet with sides, then roll the unwrapped logs in the sugar, patting it into log.

8. Transfer the log to a cutting board and slice into ½-inch-thick disks with a sharp knife.

9. Arrange the slices on the parchment-lined baking sheet, then bake until the edges are golden, or about 18–20 minutes. Transfer to wire racks to cool.

Sticky Toffee Pudding with Hot Toffee Sauce

Yield: 8–10 servings

Upon leaving Ballymaloe, I hoped to embark on my own mission to save the world from the next horrible food fad, one forgotten culinary skill at a time. A classic Irish dessert, Sticky Toffee Pudding is all about the sauce and definitely *not* a food fad. This dessert needs a lot of sauce—I mean a puddle of sauce on your plate. Every time we cook this version in class, it reminds my students of their travels in Ireland and how the taste of this dessert instantly transports them back to the Emerald Isle.

1. Preheat the oven to 350°F.

2. Soak the dates in hot tea for 15 minutes. Line the bottom and sides of a 9-inch springform pan with removable base (or a heavy cake tin) with parchment paper.

3. In a large mixing bowl, cream together the butter, brown sugar, and molasses until light and fluffy. Beat in the eggs, one at a time. Add the vanilla and coffee extracts and stir to combine.

4. Sift the flour, salt, baking powder, and baking soda into a separate bowl. Add the dry ingredients to the wet ingredients. Lastly, stir in the date and tea mixture.

5. Pour the batter into the lined tin and cook for 40–50 minutes, or until a skewer comes out clean.

6. To serve, cut into squares and ladle on loads of Hot Toffee Sauce (recipe follows). Topping each slice with a dollop of freshly whipped cream is totally appropriate here, too.

1 cup dates, chopped

1 ¼ cups brewed Ceylon tea

½ cup butter, softened

½ cup brown sugar

1 teaspoon molasses

3 eggs

1 teaspoon pure vanilla extract

1 teaspoon coffee extract

1 ½ cups all-purpose flour

½ teaspoon salt

1 ½ teaspoons baking powder

1 teaspoon baking soda

Hot Toffee Sauce

Yield: 1 ½ cups sauce

1. Combine the butter and the brown sugar in a heavy-bottomed saucepan and melt gently on a low heat.

2. Simmer for about 5 minutes, remove from the heat, and gradually stir in the cream and the vanilla extract.

3. Place the pan back on low heat and stir for 2–3 minutes, or until the sauce is absolutely smooth. Pour into a serving pitcher until ready to use. The sauce can be refrigerated for up to 1 month.

½ cup butter

¾ cup dark brown sugar

1 cup heavy whipping cream

½ teaspoon pure vanilla extract

Rhubarb Compote with Lemon Verbena

Yield: 6 pints

Note that this is a decidedly tart rendition of rhubarb sauce, and your taste buds may crave a little more sugar. Add additional ½-cup increments after the rhubarb has broken down. The lemon verbena leaves a floral essence in its wake, but could be omitted.

16 cups rhubarb, chopped into 1-inch pieces

4–6 cups granulated cane sugar, to taste

½ cup water

4 or 5 sprigs lemon verbena

1. In a large stockpot, combine the rhubarb, sugar, and water. Bring to a bubble over medium-high heat, stirring occasionally.

2. Throw in the lemon verbena sprigs. Turn the heat down, maintaining a slight bubble, simmering gently for 1–2 hours, or until thickened to the desired consistency.

3. Taste for seasoning and add more sugar if desired. Remove and discard lemon verbena sprigs.

4. Spoon the compote into pint-sized containers and then store, covered, in the fridge for up to 1 week or in the freezer for up to 12 months.

5. Serve over vanilla ice cream, alongside pork chops, stuffed into crepes, stirred into muffin or pancake batter, or eat with a spoon.

Sweet Corn Fritters with Honey Butter

Yield: about 2 dozen fritters

My favorite Minnesota State Fair food stand is the sweet corn fritters. Make your own at home with this recipe.

3 cups lard or tallow

2 cups cooked sweet corn kernels (about 4 shucked cobs)

½ cup milk plus more for thinning, if needed

1 egg

1 tablespoon coconut oil, or something similar

1 cup all-purpose flour

2 tablespoons granulated cane sugar

1 teaspoon baking powder

½ teaspoon fine sea salt plus more for sprinkling

2 tablespoons honey

4 tablespoons butter, softened

1. Preheat lard in an electric fryer set between 350°F and 375°F. Alternately, warm a heavy kettle with high sides over medium-high heat on the stove top. Have the cover nearby to contain splatters.

2. Use a fork to break up corn kernels into a large mixing bowl. Pour milk, egg, and coconut oil over the kernels, giving it a quick stir. Add the flour, sugar, baking powder, and salt and stir to combine. If the mixture looks a little thick, add 1–2 teaspoon more of milk and mix well.

3. Drop the batter by teaspoonfuls into the hot lard. Fry for 1–2 minutes, flipping once or twice to encourage even browning. Use a slotted spoon to transfer the fritters to a paper-towel-lined plate. Lightly sprinkle with fine sea salt. Repeat with remaining batter.

4. Mix together the honey and the softened butter and serve alongside the fritters. To reheat, place the fritters on a baking sheet and warm in an oven preheated to 350°F for 7–9 minutes, or until sizzling and crispy.

Rendering Tallow

Oh, how to find eloquent enough words to describe the slightly repugnant process of rendering tallow? First off, let's begin with what tallow is. Tallow is the rendered fat that surrounds the kidneys, sometimes referred to as leaf lard, in an animal such as a cow or pig. Once rendered, the fat is very similar to lard in both looks and functionality. Tallow also has a high smoke point, which makes it ideal for deep-frying foods like french fries. In fact, up until the no-fat fad of the early 1990s, McDonald's used tallow to fry its world-famous fries. Tallow is a rich source of conjugated linoleic acid (CLA) fat, a cancer-fighting agent. Terrific! Bring on the tallow!

According to BeefTallow.com, tallow is an excellent source of niacin; vitamins B6, B12, and K2; selenium; iron; phosphorus; potassium; and riboflavin. Grass-fed beef tallow contains a high ratio of CLA, and also contains a small amount of vitamin D, similar to lard. Contrary to the popular conception, tallow is good for your health, as tallow fat is similar to the fat and muscles in the heart. Recent studies show that human beings need saturated fats like tallow and lard to keep the heart pumping and healthy.

Should you ever process a cow, make sure to have the butcher save the leaf lard, or fat surrounding the kidneys. If it's unlikely you'll process a cow soon (or ever), check with your local butcher shop or natural food co-op to see if they carry leaf lard.

Here's how to make your own tallow:

Tallow

    8 pounds leaf lard

First, chop your fat. (Sounds fun doesn't it?) I used the fat of 1 cow, about 8 pounds of leaf lard total. You'll need a sharp knife with a longish blade. The cutting board is going to take on a, ahem, shall we say greasy patina. Don't worry—it'll wash off, but I'd advise against using a porous cutting board. The smaller the chop, the better the rendering. Aim for 1-inch cubes. When you're chopping, try to remove any remaining tendons in the lard.

Now, throw your chopped leaf lard into a big oven-proof pot. Preheat your oven to 375°F and get ready to have your house smell like slightly burnt cow fat. It's alright. Your family won't mind. They surely will notice the plumes of smoke coming from the oven, asking, "What's going on in the kitchen?" You might try to torture them by assuring them not to worry, it's just supper cooking.

After the fat cooks for about 90 minutes, you'll check on it to see what looks like state fair cheese curds! Pierce these with a sharp object to release all deliciousness. When you're done rendering, save these crispy bits to eat like cracklin'.

Strain your hot tallow into a large vessel, then quickly pour into widemouthed jars or some other airtight vessel. The tallow sets up quickly, so you need to move fast. Tallow will keep in a refrigerator for up to six months and in a freezer for up to one year.

ABOUT THE AUTHOR

Becki Melvie is a trained chef, small business owner, cooking class instructor, and Proverbs 31 woman. Her mission is to help families have wholesome food with convenience. She lives in Buffalo, Minnesota with her husband and two boys. Meet up with her on social on Facebook and Instagram: @TheAbundantKitchen.